3 4028 09099 1234
HARRIS COUNTY PUBLIC LIBRARY

J 636.753 Boz
Bozzo, Lind
I like dachshunds

W9-BYJ-271

WITHDRAWN

$9.35
ocn950611478

DOGS

I LIKE

# DACHSHUNDS!

Linda Bozzo

It is the Mission of the American Canine Association (ACA) to provide registered dog owners with the educational support needed for raising, training, showing, and breeding the healthiest pets expected by responsible pet owners throughout the world. Through our activities and services, we encourage and support the dog world in order to promote best-known husbandry standards as well as to ensure that the voice and needs of our customers are quickly and properly addressed.

Our continued support, commitment, and direction are guided by our customers, including veterinary, legal, and legislative advisors. ACA aims to provide the most efficient, cooperative, and courteous service to our customers and strives to set the standard for education and problem solving for all who depend on our services.

For more information, please visit www.acacanines.com, e-mail customerservice@acadogs.com, phone 1-800-651-8332, or write to the American Canine Association at PO Box 121107, Clermont, FL 34712.

Published in 2017 by Enslow Publishing, LLC.
101 W. 23rd Street, Suite 240, New York, NY 10011

Copyright © 2017 by Enslow Publishing, LLC.

All rights reserved.

No part of this book may be reproduced by any means without the written permission of the publisher.

**Library of Congress Cataloging-in-Publication Data**
Names: Bozzo, Linda, author.
Title: I like dachshunds! / Linda Bozzo.
Description: New York, NY : Enslow Publishing, 2017. | Series: Discover dogs with the American Canine Association | Includes bibliographical references and index. | Audience: Ages 5 and up. | Audience: Grades K to grade 3.
Identifiers: LCCN 2016020283 | ISBN 9780766081635 (library bound) | ISBN 9780766081611 (pbk.) | ISBN 9780766081628 (6-pack)
Subjects: LCSH: Dachshunds—Juvenile literature.
Classification: LCC SF429.D25 B69 2017 | DDC 636.753/8--dc23
LC record available at https://lccn.loc.gov/2016020283

Printed in China

**To Our Readers:** We have done our best to make sure all websites in this book were active and appropriate when we went to press. However, the author and the publisher have no control over and assume no liability for the material available on those websites or on any websites they may link to. Any comments or suggestions can be sent by e-mail to customerservice@enslow.com.

**Photo Credits:** Cover, p. 1 Alex Vinci/Shutterstock.com; p. 3 (left) © iStockphoto.com/dageldog; p. 3 (right) John Madere/Corbis/Getty Images; p. 5 ch ch/Shutterstock.com; p. 6 Annmarie Young/Shutterstock.com; p. 9 Hannamariah/Shutterstock.com; p. 10 Håkan Dahlström/Moment/Getty Images; p. 13 (top) © iStockphoto.com/WilleeCole; p 13 (bottom) © iStockphoto.com/jclegg (collar), Luisa Leal Photography/Shutterstock.com (bed), gvictoria/Shutterstock.com (brush), In-Finity/Shutterstock.com (dishes), © iStockphoto.com/Lisa Thornberg (leash, toys); p. 14 (left) Liliya Kulianionak/Shutterstock.com; p. 14 (right) © iStockphoto.com/mykeyruna; p. 15 Tannis Toohey/Toronto Star/Getty Images; p. 17 Teresa Lett/Moment Open/Getty Images; p. 18 Blend Images - JGI/Tom Grill/Brand X Pictures/Getty Images; p. 19 James Tarver/Flickr Flash/Getty Images; p. 21 Hannamariah/Shutterstock.com; p. 22 © iStockphoto.com/Antagain.

**Enslow Publishing**
101 W. 23rd Street
Suite 240
New York, NY 10011
USA

enslow.com

# CONTENTS

IS A DACHSHUND RIGHT
FOR YOU?  4

A DOG OR A PUPPY?  7

LOVING YOUR DACHSHUND  8

EXERCISE  11

FEEDING YOUR
DACHSHUND  12

GROOMING  15

WHAT YOU SHOULD KNOW
ABOUT DACHSHUNDS 16

A GOOD FRIEND  19

NOTE TO PARENTS  20

WORDS TO KNOW  22

READ ABOUT DOGS  23

INDEX  24

# IS A DACHSHUND RIGHT FOR YOU?

Dachshunds do well in any size home. They are great with children and like being with other dogs. If you already own a dog, a dachshund might be a good choice for you.

Dachshunds come in two sizes: standard and miniature.

# A DOG OR A PUPPY?

Dachshunds are very smart. They are also stubborn. So training a dachshund puppy will take patience and time. If you do not have time to train a puppy, an older dachshund may be better for your family.

Grown up dachshunds are small in size.

# LOVING YOUR DACHSHUND

Dachshunds, with their short legs and long bodies, are easy to love. Your dachshund will want to be a part of everything your family does.

# EXERCISE

Dachshunds like jumping and playing games like **fetch**. A walk using a **leash** is great exercise for this dog. Dachshunds like to be kept busy!

A dachshund's long back can be easily injured when playing.

# FEEDING YOUR DACHSHUND

Dachshunds are good eaters.

Dogs can be fed wet or dry dog food. Ask a **veterinarian (vet)**, a doctor for animals, which food is best for your dachshund and how much to feed her.

Give your dachshund fresh, clean water every  day.

Remember to keep your dog's food and water dishes clean. Dirty dishes can make a dog sick.

Do not feed your dog people food.
It can make her sick.

Your new dog will need:

a collar with a tag

a bed

a brush

food and water dishes

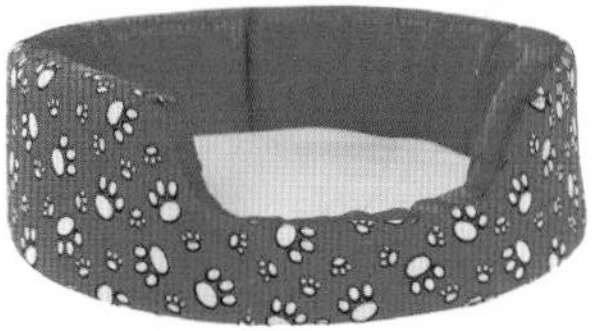

a leash

toys

Dachshunds come in three types of coats: smooth coat (also known as short-haired), long-haired, and wirehaired.

# GROOMING

All dachshunds **shed**, some more than others. Long-haired dachshunds may need baths more often than short-haired and wirehaired dachshunds.

Use a gentle soap made just for dogs.

A dachshund's nails need to be clipped. A vet or **groomer** can show you how. Your dog's ears should be cleaned and their teeth should be brushed by an adult.

# WHAT YOU SHOULD KNOW ABOUT DACHSHUNDS

Dachshunds can be barkers and diggers. They are good with other dogs but not with other small animals. Dachshunds are good watch dogs. They like to protect their families.

Healthy standard dachshunds can live to be 16 years old. Miniatures can live as long as 19 years.

Dachshunds were bred
to be hunters.

You will need to take your new dog to the vet for a checkup. He will need shots, called vaccinations, and yearly checkups to keep him healthy. If you think your dog may be sick or hurt, call your vet.

# A GOOD FRIEND

Your dachshund will be a good friend for a long time. This brave dog will enjoy being by your side for many years.

The hot dog we know today was once called a "dachshund" sausage after the dachshund dog.

# NOTE TO PARENTS

It is important to consider having your dog spayed or neutered when the dog is young. Spaying and neutering are operations that prevent unwanted puppies and can help improve the overall health of your dog.

It is also a good idea to microchip your dog, in case he or she gets lost. A vet will implant a microchip under the skin containing an identification number that can be scanned at a vet's office or animal shelter. The microchip registry is contacted and the company uses the ID number to look up your information from a database.

Some towns require licenses for dogs, so be sure to check with your town clerk.

For more information, speak with a vet.

There are many dogs, young and old, waiting to be adopted from animal shelters and rescue groups.

**fetch**  To go after a toy and bring it back.

**groomer**  A person who bathes and brushes dogs.

**leash**  A chain or strap that attaches to the dog's collar.

**shed**  When dog hair falls out so new hair can grow.

**vaccinations**  Shots that dogs need to stay healthy.

**veterinarian (vet)** A doctor for animals.

## Books

Finne, Stephanie. *Dachshunds*. Minneapolis, MN: Abdo
    Publishing, 2015.

Schuh, Mari C. *Dachshunds*. Minneapolis, MN: Bellwether
    Media, 2016.

## Websites

**American Canine Association Inc., Kids Corner**
acakids.com
*Visit the official website of the American Canine Association.*

**National Geographic for Kids, Pet Central**
kids.nationalgeographic.com/explore/pet-central/
*Learn more about dogs and other pets at the official site of the
National Geographic Society for Kids.*

Harris County Public Library
Houston, Texas

## B
back, 11
barkers, 16
bath, 15
bed, 13
brush, 13

## C
checkup, 18
children, 4
cleanliness, 12
collar, 13

## D
dachshunds
  coat types, 14, 15
  lifespan, 16
  and other animals, 4, 16
  size, 4, 7
  temperament, 7, 16, 19
  who should get one, 4
diggers, 16
dishes, 12, 13

## E
ears, 15
exercise, 11

## F
fence,
fetch, 11
food, 12, 13

## G
grooming, 15

## H
hot dog, 19
hunters, 17

## L
leash, 11, 13

## M
microchip, 20

## N
nails, 15
neutering, 20

## S
shedding, 15
spaying, 20
supplies for your new pet, 13

## T
teeth, 15
toys, 13
training, 7

## V
vaccinations, 18
veterinarian, 12, 15, 18, 20

## W
watch dogs, 16
water, 12, 13